Recovery Thinking,
90-Days to Change Your Life!

By Daniel Callahan, LMSW

Table of Contents

*** Conclusion, Thank you…

Acknowledgements

I must be honest today I consider myself the most blessed man in the world. I live a happy and joyous recovered life. It was not always that way. The principles in this book came from many years of experience both positive and negative. There are so many people that have been vital parts of this journey it is nearly impossible to name them all. For those I fail to mention my apologies, I thank you for being a part of my life past, present or future!

First and foremost is my family, my mom and dad shaped me into the person I have become. Their commitments to community service lead me to a profession in human service. My sister Tracy has remained a rock for me through thick and thin she never once gave up on me! My brother "Pie" and sister Peggy I love dearly.

I have been blessed with four awesome kids: Sean, Kristin, Liam and Seamus. I am so proud to be their dad. Sean is my business partner and friend today something I could only have dreamed of when he was born. Kristin blessed us with a baby boy "Joey" in 2010, Liam attends college a few miles away at Florida Atlantic University and my youngest Seamus lives with me and attends high school.

I would be negligent if I did not thank Laura "Petey" Pettersen, Liam and Seamus' mom. Besides being a great mom Laura proofed every paper for me when I began college. Without her I would not have written this book. Let me fill you in, I was anything but an English scholar when I began!

I had two sponsors that helped shape my recovery foundation. Without them I do not believe I would be the man I am today. Thank you George N. and Joe O. My most recent sponsor is better labeled my friend and Mentor Jack Jackson. Jack has touched more lives and continues to do so more than any other human being I know!

Today I have four business partners: My son Sean, Rick Glaser, Ryan Garmley and Keith Houlihan. They are my friends and I trust and respect each of them.

I have been influenced by several people via mentorship, reading of their work, listening to their audios and as colleagues or my supervisor on the job. I would love to tell you that everything I write is unique and solely my own. But that is wrong, nothing is unique everything is copied from some lessons I have learned throughout the years. The key is they work because I utilize everything I suggest. I simply recorded these lessons through the years. I am sure that I will miss giving credit where credit is due, however this is purely coincidental and not a slight! I offer my apologies in advance.

So in no particular order Thank you: Diane Johnson, Carolyn Peabody, Ellen Healion, Kathy Rogers, Earl Nightingale, Tony Robbins, Art Williams, Jimmy Meyers, Joe O'Sullivan, Bob Safford, Sr., George Nealis, Joe Ensor, Joe Vitale, John Addison, Napoleon Hill, Pat Williams, Jesus, John Maxwell, Paul Gulbronson, Jack Canfield, Mike Nearney, Joel Osteen, Duff McGee, Robert Kiyosaki, Donald Trump, Joyce Meyer, Betty Kelly, Bro. Jack Moylan, and so many many more!

Finally the love of my life Diana Patricia! Te amo!

Recovery Thinking, *90-Days to Change Your Life!*

Positive meaningful recovery is living life to it's fullest. Living a Purposeful Clean and Sober Life takes focusing on what we want and not solely on our challenges! Changing the way we think takes focus, diligence, and daily discipline. Recovery Thinking leads the reader through 90 days of changing the way you think on a daily basis.

My name is Dan Callahan I have recovered from alcoholism and addiction. As I look back on my addiction history, I consider myself a teenaged-addict. I have no recollection of when I had my first drink of alcohol. I do remember my first experience with marijuana. It was the summer between Elementary school (grade 6) and Jr. High (grade 7). It didn't take long before I was completely out of control. My life completely revolved around "The Party". I would walk to school usually alone and smoke a joint on the way in every day! I wanted people to smell the reefer on my clothing. I took it as a sign of "coolness". I was no longer the square peg trying to fit into the round hole!

I used drugs and alcohol until I was nearly 28 years old. I went through phases from hallucinogens to "Benzo's" to Cocaine, Pain Killers, "Crank" you name I would take it. I spent three years in prison from the age of 20 to 23. I was heading towards destruction quickly. Finally, on April 14, 1988 I surrendered and began the recovery journey. I followed every suggestion that was made to me by my support group. I got a sponsor; I completed and utilized the steps and principles of recovery, and I changed the way I think, act and do things.

I returned to college and attained a Masters Degree from Fordham University. I chose the helping profession and became a social worker. But the most important choice I made beyond my relationship with God was centered on my thinking. I decided that I needed to change completely, and thoroughly how I thought. I was a negative person; I always sought to prove why you were "wrong". I always looked at the glass half empty. I would look for the catch in everything. I would hear people talk about hearing the birds chirp in the morning and I would think they were too noisy!

Finally in 1998, ten years after I began the journey I was introduced to a new way of thinking beyond positive thinking. I started to study material based upon self-improvement. I had been trained and believed that focusing on my strengths was more important than overcoming my weaknesses. But, in practice I fell short of the mark. I stopped reading material that focused on what is wrong with me and how to overcome it. I started focusing on what is right with me and how to be better!

This may not sound like much but it is a huge difference. I put these essays together over the course of the past few years. They are intended to be guides to help us change the way we think. To live happy, joyous and free we must begin to think differently. We must live life to the fullest!

Living life to it's fullest….

We are here for just a flicker! In the scheme of things our 75 to 100 years is nothing, it flies by. We need to make the most of it, every single day. We all have our talents, dreams, desires, wants, likes and dislikes. Evaluating them and compiling a Mission and Vision is the start of attaining and living a life to fulfill our purpose. Anything else is a waste!

Wow what a direct and bold statement. Ok take a second and think back, have you ever said to yourself or someone else, "what is this all about?" What is life about? Why am I here? What do I want to do in my life? What do I want to be when I grow up? If you answer yes to any of these questions you have questioned your purpose. You have what every reasonably minded person that I know of has, a desire to be, do and have. That is human nature! That is also what God wants of you. God wants you to become a better you!

So where do you start? First is to practice the A B C 's of a successful and joyous life:

A) **Always Be Positive,** follow the three rules of a positive mental attitude: 1) Always Be Positive, 2) Always Be Positive, 3) Always Be Positive!

B) Be a Student of Life; never ever stop growing. Read, listen to audio programs that are educational in nature, live, learn and love.

C) Cheerlead your friends, family and co-workers! Always offer praise to people but never offer praise if it is not due, yet keep the negatives to your self. Be happy for other people's accomplishments.

Life is meant to be enjoyed and not to be endured. That is the key to reasonable happiness. I found the key to success. The key to change and to master living life to it's fullest. What is it you ask? Follow the Three rules to happiness:

Rule # 1 Always Be Positive
Rule # 2 Always Be Positive
Rule # 3 Always Be Positive

Enjoy the Journey Because Life is Good!

How to use the book:

There is no one particular way to read this book. The idea is to use it on a daily basis for at least 90 days and then start over. Read one essay per day in the evening before you go to bed. Many of us go to bed after watching the evening news. That is a mistake. We go to bed full of negativity and sleep on that. If you read an essay prior to retiring for the night you go to bed with a positive message resonating through the night. I also suggest you read through the book once in its entirety over the course of a few days. But the ultimate choice is yours utilize it how you see fit! No matter what your choice, I thank you for the confidence you have placed in me by purchasing this material. I take that seriously and I hope and pray that you will take these essays and lessons seriously so that you too will enjoy a happy, clean and sober life!

Go, Go, Go…

Dan Callahan ☺

A Word on Alcoholics Anonymous (AA)

Before we start let me say a word about AA (Alcoholics Anonymous). First this material is not an endorsement for AA nor does AA endorse this material. However, I would be in the wrong not to discuss how I think, feel and believe about AA.

Bill W. & Dr Bob S.

Alcoholics Anonymous (AA) is one of the most misunderstood programs on the face of this earth. First AA is not just a program, AA has a program it utilizes it is referred to as the "Twelve Step Approach". AA is more than a program it is a fellowship. What is a fellowship? Mutual support and a little bit more. Many AA members become great friends with other members. Often guys and gals meet each other when they begin the recovery journey in AA.

The knock on AA is often the idea of going to meetings forever, some people will ask, "do I have to do this forever"? My question to them is, "do what forever"? Have friends that like you that trust you and care about you, that you like, trust and care about? Build lifelong relationships that are productive and fulfilling? The reason people ask these questions is simple, they simply do not know or understand the power of fellowship with like minded positive people that are heading in the same direction as we are now heading.

What is all this talk about the twelve steps? Quite frankly the twelve step approach is a spiritual model of recovery that enables the participant to address the fact that they need help overcoming alcoholism and in many cases addiction, repairing the damage done to self, friends, family and others, developing a new strategy for living a moral, happy and drug free life, amending ones actions and living a renewed life free of guilt, remorse, shame and discontinuing the damaging cycle of drunkenness and or addiction.

It is all about the results! AA in its early days boasted a 75% success ratio with what has been termed "low bottom drunks". These were mostly men and some women that were physically and mentally addicted to alcohol. Friends', family and professionals considered many of them "hopeless cases". But when they began attending, fellowshipping and working the AA program they were freed of the bondage that alcohol had on their lives. Today although there is no real way to know what the recovery rate truly is, it is apparently lower than 75%. Some people state that it is approximately a 10% success rate.

Well that is not success if you are using my standards. So why has the success rate changed through the years so drastically? There are many theories, some people believe that because people are often coerced into treatment by family, employers, the courts etc… they are not really there for themselves and do not take the steps or the idea of the program or fellowship seriously. Other people believe that because people come to AA before they hit a deep enough bottom, they only stick their toes in the water to test it out and therefore do not take the process seriously.

Whatever your take may be on the failure rate, the truth is simple, if you want to get and stay sober you can if you take action. It is not AA that will fail you or your family, it is you that will fail you, but only if you allow yourself to fail. The honest fact is this, if you make a commitment to recover, you will recover. Change the way you think, stop asking why it does not work and start by asking, "how can it work for me"?

With AA you can recover!

Once you recover, continue to do the things that helped you to overcome alcoholism. Build a life that is filled with sober friends. Always be working on self-improvement, setting goals to be the best you can possibly be, and keep helping others to do the same. Be a living example of positive recovery, AA works if you work it, so work it!!!

Go, Go, Go…

Dan ☺

Success Leaves Clues

"If you could find out what the most successful people did in any area and then you did the same thing over and over, you'd eventually get the same result they do." — *Brian Tracy*

The key to recovery is simple, do what those of us that are successful getting and living recovered lives do and you will get and stay sober. Extremely simple! Not always easy but it is simple. I received a message from an individual this morning. She said she was frustrated and disheartened about her progress. She stated that she felt let down. She believed that the things she needed to do, change career, people, and the places she frequented and she would have a better life! She said she was frustrated because she did not feel that way after three months.

The truth is that recovery takes work. Nothing is easy; in fact if it's easy it's sleazy. Recovery takes work for some of us it takes grinding it out until we see the light at the end of the tunnel. I often worry when I hear that things are awesome for the 90-day wonders. If we are not stretched a bit when it comes time down the road that stress arises and it will arise we may snap. So stress and challenges are our friends.

In the beginning of my journey I would compare myself to others and think "WHY ME"? Today I know why me, I needed the challenges at the outset to become the human being I am today. Today when I make a mistake I dust off and move on, that cannot be said for some of those people I envied in the beginning!

For the young lady that sent me the note I want to encourage you to fight the fight, keep the faith, stare adversity in the face and say F U… I am mad as hell and I am not gonna take it anymore! Life is good!!!

Go, Go, Go…

Dan ☺

Turn Deficiencies into Strengths!

"Face your deficiencies and acknowledge them; but do not let them master you. Let them teach you patience, sweetness, insight." – *Helen Keller*

Over the course of time my deficiencies have turned out to be my strengths. I was always a fidgety kid, got into all kinds of trouble because I was always into something. I was persistent and stubborn and just wouldn't quit. I would drive my mother crazy if I wanted something because I simply did not hear the word "NO". Well I heard it but I did not comprehend it. I thought it meant "not now". At times I thought it meant "ask me differently". Sometimes I thought it meant "yes but you must keep asking"!

That attitude has put me into some tight spots but it has also built my determination and desire to never quit. When I realized that alcohol and drugs were causing me problems I attempted to fix it. I spent eight years trying to do it my own way. People thought I would never make it because I couldn't follow the path of least resistance. That often causes people to quit on themselves and get frustrated, but not me. I wanted to be somebody so badly that I kept at it! I simply would not quit.

Today I am grateful that I am a fighter. I have turned a deficiency into a strength. Today I recognize that life is good and well worth the fight!

Go, Go, Go…

Dan :)

#1 Investment is You

When it comes to taking your life to the next level of success invest in you! In the ABC's of the Recovered Life B stands for "Be a Student of Life". In order to grow into the person we are we must work at it. We must always be improving. To do that we must invest in ourselves wisely, we must spend time getting better, do the work it takes and take life seriously. Here are three principles to help you to grow and become a better you.

1) Build a strong commitment to you and the recovery community. In order to recover it is imperative that we are not alone in the trenches. We need mutual support from those folks that have been where we are. Having a support group, sponsor and commitment to the program is key to long term recovery, abstinence and joy.

2) Be Foolish! Yes that is correct, in order to get better we must be willing to do the things that we feel foolish about. Building our confidence takes a willingness to follow suggestions no matter how foolish they seem. Affirmations are key to joy in the long term. Yet it feels funny affirming that we are positive, joyful and a winner to name a few. Often in the beginning we feel like a fraud. But we need to allow ourselves to be foolish in order to get to a place where we are winners in life!

3) Passion on the side. We must live with passion. We all have a purpose in this world. People that are happier are people that live with passion and purpose. If you are working a job you dislike or in a career that is not congruent with your purpose, then nurture your passion on the side. Keep it alive within until you can position yourself to live it fully!

Go, Go, Go…

Dan ☺

The Land of the Living.

"Death is not the greatest loss in life, the greatest loss is what dies in us while we are still alive."
- Norman Cousins

 Addiction and alcoholism rob us of every fiber of life while we are actively using or drinking. **We become the walking dead.** I remember walking into the rooms and hearing "welcome to the land of the living". I knew immediately what they were saying because I was the epitome of the walking dead. I remember as a teenager when my uncle took me to the Veterans Hospital. There were men walking around the grounds and on the wards that were out of it. I asked him what happened to them and he responded that they ruined their minds by drinking too much.

That vision stayed with me forever. I remember thinking to myself in my lowest of low days that I was not going to die I was going to live a long and miserable life! Today in hindsight, I was right about one thing, I was not going to die! Today I live a happy, joyous and free life. I am grateful that recovery held it's arms wide open for me. I love life and enjoy sharing it with anyone that is willing to listen, because life is good!

Go, Go, Go…

Dan :)

Gratitude

Develop an attitude of gratitude, and give thanks for everything that happens to you, knowing that every step forward is a step toward achieving something bigger and better than your current situation.
-- Brian Tracy

Every time I sit to write I find myself thinking, now this is important! This is everything! When I write about leadership I think leadership is everything. When I write about Joy, I think Joy is everything. This morning as I am writing about "Gratitude" I think gratitude is everything!

I wonder how many times I have said, "now this is everything". The truth is that there are so many important things in life that overflow and mesh with each other to help us create a life worth living. Life is good and we can make it better and better and better by putting in the effort to make it so. We can choose to live a day at a time enjoying life as it comes, enduring life as it is or we can work at personal development and make it better!

Gratitude is essential for us in the recovered life. An attitude of gratitude will help get you through the tough times. They say tough times don't last but tough people do! Our toughness comes from our hope, our hope stems from gratitude!

Live, life, well!

Go, Go, Go...

Dan :)

Aversive Prevention

I was recently asked for the treatment protocol for "Hangovers". I guess people need to know how to combat this ancient malady. It has been many years, decades in fact that I have considered returning to drunkenness. The cure for the hangover was clear very early on in my recovery, **abstinence.**

However, when the thought emerged to drink here is what I would do; I would drive to the ATM take out as much cash as I could from the machine, write a check for more, and then return to my home. I would crumble all of my money and toss it into the toilet and flush! Then I would gorge my self with the food I hated the most usually fish sticks till I would vomit all over myself. Defecate and urinate in my pants, lay on the bathroom floor with the heat at the highest levels possible after slamming my head on the floor to replicate the wonderful feeling of solace I would have the morning after...

Go, Go, Go...

Dan :)

The A. B. C.'s

"Be aware of wonder. Live a balanced life — learn some and think some and draw and paint and sing and dance and play and work every day some." – *Robert Fulghum*

I love sharing my experience, strength and hope on a daily basis through writing. Once, I was winding down in school, took on some extra work and playing catch-up on some things that I fell behind on, so I had been a bit slow in my writing when I came upon this quote. It motivated me to action. We must be aware of the wonder around us. Living a balanced life is essential in recovery. We should be cautious not to get too hungry, angry, lonely or tired, HALT! We are best served when we live the ABC's of the recovered life.

A: Always be positive...
B: Be a student of life...
C: Cheerlead others...

Life is way too good to be mediocre, live life well!!!!

Go, Go, Go...

Dan :)

"A" Always Be Positive

There are three basic rules of success, Rule number one, Always Be Positive. Rule number Two, Always Be Positive. Rule number Three, Always Be Positive.

Many folks hear statements like these and turn a deaf ear. They conjure up images of some pretentious geek playing Mr. Happy! If that is what you think then please stop and reconsider. Positive-ity is a state of mind that a majority of us need to consciously work on. We are conditioned to think negative. Many people have an alternative term to justify negativity. They call it constructive thinking. They say you must challenge all thought, suggestion and theory with critical thinking!

What a load of bad B.S. ("Belief System", Dan Ohler)! Obviously we all must "Stop, Look and Listen" for the train when we cross the railroad. However, we must be cautious about sending down the warning signal prematurely.

So what does one do to acquire a positive mental attitude? First start the day off in a positive tone. Here are some suggestions I use, add as many as you can you are not limited to one:

1) Up lifting positive music.
2) Prayer with praise and thanksgiving.
3) Daily meditation or spiritual book.
4) If you live with your life partner a hug and a kiss and an uplifting comment to them.
5) If you have children a hug and a kiss and an encouraging word.
6) Yes to life! I hit the shower to; I'm alive I'm awake and I feel great!
7) A good healthy breakfast.
8) An expectation of a positive and productive day.
9) A moment of reflection for everything I am grateful for receiving and accepting.

Expect a positive outcome and you will achieve positive results. If you focus on the negative or constructive thought process, well as they say, "Suffer Well"!
Go. Go, Go...

Dan ☺

B, Be a student of life.

"I teach something called The Law of Probabilities, which says the more things you try, the more likely one of them will work. The more books you read, the more likely one of them will have an answer to a question that could solve the major problems of your life, make you wealthier, solve a health problem, whatever it might be." -- *Jack Canfield*

B, Be a student of life.

We should always be learning and growing. The more positive information we add to our arsenal the better equipped we are to handle stress, answer questions we have, solve our life challenges, and live life joyfully. When we stay active learning we build strength in living our daily lives. Reading and learning gives us an internal library that is a tool to develop successful life strategies.

The more we learn the stronger our self-esteem becomes. Positivity permeates our belief system. Possibility thinking gains strength and is rooted in factual knowledge rather than simply blind faith. If we are to become all that we can become as human beings we need to "Be a Student of Life"! Life is good!!!

Go, Go, Go…

Dan :)

BBBBB

"One hour per day of study will put you at the top of your field within three years. Within five years you'll be a national authority. In seven years, you can be one of the best people in the world at what you do."
— *Earl Nightingale*

We minimize our capacity and ability to learn, grow and become all that we are gifted to become. In the A, B, C's of the recovered life, "B" is **"Be a student of life"**. As I teach newcomers to the world of recovery these principles I am often greeted with a look of perplexity. They sometimes respond that they are not in high school and are not interested in going back. But this is a shortsighted view of life and the power of growth and development.

I can speak on this for hours however, I know this for sure. We must be always improving in our lives. We must be filled with passion for life. We must live within our purpose, more specifically, within our God given talents. Many people come to me and want more therapy, therapy does not get or keep you sober, recovery does, and you do! If it was therapy alcoholism and addiction would not be as prevalent as it is, probably more pointedly relapse would not be as prevalent.

If you want what we have, do what we do! Mutual supports, admit, atone, forgive, focus on others and live with passion! Anything else is theory...

Life is good...

Go, Go, Go...

Dan :)

Cheerlead Others!

"Every day, tell at least one person something you like, admire, or appreciate about them."
- Richard Carlson

C. Cheerlead others!

Spreading the joy to others is a great thing to do. I love to help people see and reach their potential. When we feel good about ourselves we are more apt to do the work and stretch ourselves to make it happen! Mary Kay Ash once said that everyone has a flashing sign across his or her chest that says MAKE ME FEEL SPECIAL! Think about that, not only do I want to feel good about life, others and me but so does everyone else!

Help people see the good in themselves. Be appreciative for everyone's contribution to the world. Find the aspect of their life to commend rather than criticize. Life is way too good to allow it to pass us by. Live life well!

Go, Go, Go…

Dan :)

Powerful!

This I know. This I believe with all my heart. If we want a free and peaceful world, if we want to make the deserts bloom and man to grow to greater dignity as a human being ... we can do it. -- *Eleanor Roosevelt*

A positive mental attitude enhances our ability to achieve anything we want to achieve. Many of us take the word powerless completely out of context. We are powerless in a clash of wills with other people. If we are blessed with the condition of being an alcoholic or addict we are powerless over alcohol and other mind-altering substances. But we have much more power in life than we think we have.

The truth is, we become what we think about most. What we focus on, believe and attach feeling to we become. That means that if we truly want something, if we simply believe we can attain it, we will get it. We are not the center of the universe but we have much more power than we think we have. This includes recovery, which entails, a life of happiness, joy and freedom!

Life is good!

Go, Go, Go...

Dan :)

Into Action!

"One of the great tragedies of life is that men seldom bridge the gulf between practice and profession, between doing and saying." --*Martin Luther King, Jr.*

The greatest frustration is when I see or hear a newcomer share that they are struggling. If asked I always remind them that this too shall pass. The other day someone said that the month after he hit his 90 days was terrible. He said he wanted to use and was miserable. I asked him what he did the first 90 days to be successful? Of course he knew exactly what he did and he told me. I asked the obvious question, are you still doing those things? Well you know the answer, right after the "yeah buts" he said, "you are right I stopped my prayer, meditation and affirmations"! Rocket science!

The greatest tragedy is when we know what to do but just don't do it! We need to bridge the gap between knowledge and action. If we want to be happy, joyous and free we must do what happy, joyous and free recovered people do! Simple… Life is good!

Go, Go, Go…

Dan :)

Messenger of Hope

"They may forget what you said, but they will never forget how you made them feel." - *Carl W. Buechner*

I had to remind myself of the reason I do what I do. My purpose, my vision, my desire is to make the world a better place. For a very long time I did not see my role clearly enough. Sure I am good, maybe even pretty damn good at what I do, which is: I help to make people feel special and be a catalyst for positive change in people's lives. But somewhere underneath it all is the radio station "WIFM" (What's In It For Me) playing between my two ears. Sometimes the volume plays so loud that I will believe my own press! But at the end of the day when I look in the mirror I am what I am called to be, a messenger of hope. Just a fellow that has been saved from the bondage of addiction trying to make the world a better place!

Today I will walk' talk and act like the person I am striving to be. Today I will put in the effort and give my all to the cause. Today I will do my best to make the world a better place. I cannot fail, I will not fail, I have been given this gift of sobriety, I will give it back. Life is good!!!

Go, Go, Go…

Dan :)

Do What Drives You

"The one piece of advice I can give you is, do what turns you on. Do something that if you had all the money in the world, you'd still be doing it. You've got to have a reason to jump out of bed in the morning." — *Warren Buffett*

Our world has changed significantly over the years. With it our attitude and view of life has changed as well. For many people no longer is it acceptable to go get a job that has benefits and retirement, commit to the thirty year plan and retire with a 401K and pension. In fact on average a person will change their careers and or employment 6 times during their life span.

I may have been a little before my time but I remember at 18 when my family wanted to help me get a job with my fathers company. I turned it down. It did not go over too well! I just couldn't see myself in that grind. I had no clue what I wanted to do but I knew it wasn't that!

We need to do what drives us. Security is a fallacy today, a company will cut thousands of workers over a poor set of quarters, and there is no employer-employee loyalty any longer. What matters is that we use our God given talents to the best of our ability. We do the work that is in alignment with our strengths. This is what gives us the reason to jump out of bed in the morning; this is where our passion lies! Life is good!!!

Go, Go, Go…

Dan :)

Risk It!

"To try is to risk failure. But risk must be taken because the greatest hazard of life is to risk nothing. The person who risks nothing does nothing, has nothing, is nothing. He may avoid suffering and sorrow, but he simply cannot learn, feel, change, grow, live, and love." -- *Leo Buscaglia*

The greatest risk I took was the day I reached out for help. I had attempted to get help in the past but I did not commit to the process. I half-assed it hoping that things would change. I could not imagine life without partying. The only aspect of the message I ever heard was, "you can NEVER drink or drug again"! I couldn't grasp the idea of "NEVER".

Finally in 1988 I was so sick and tired of my continued failure and let downs in my life that I surrendered. I took the risk to commit to one day at a time asking God to help me stay clean. To work the steps, to implement the principles of recovery into my life, and to build friendship with others that are heading in the same direction with the same goal as me, FREEDOM!

I took the plunge with very little reservation. The only reservation I carried was the fear of taking a personal inventory and sharing it with another human being. But that was quickly extinguished when my sponsor asked me. "What is the worst thing you have ever done in your life"? I knew I was sober when I answered him. I took the risk and boy I am glad I did. Life is good!

Go, Go, Go…

Dan :)

Power of Belief

"I have learned, as a rule of thumb, never to ask whether you can do something. Say, instead, that you are doing it. Then fasten your seat belt. The most remarkable things follow." – *Julia Cameron*

The journey is remarkable if I allow it to be. I am a huge believer in the power of belief! When I believe that all is well, I live in harmony and acceptance. When I try to control and keep things in my life aligned and in order I am out of congruence with a peaceful, joyful, and sober minded man. In early recovery this was the case more often than not. I remember thinking if I can just get through this I will be okay!

The truth is, I am okay all the time but I must believe that. "It" always works out. Life is always good. God is good. When I believe these truths in my life I am effective as a teacher, coach, father, employee, partner, and every other role I fill. I love life, I love the recovered life and I am excited about the future as well as today!

Life is exciting!

Go, Go, Go…

Dan :)

Go For It!

"The mass of men lead lives of quiet desperation and go to the grave with the song still in them."
— *Henry David Thoreau*

Go for it! We are all here for a purpose; we all have natural strengths, likes, dislikes and desires. We need to continue to cultivate our strengths and do what we are good at and enjoy. Too many people live the grind giving no thought to the song that lies within their hearts. We are only here for a flicker of time. Recovery is our opportunity to get up and grow into our full potential.

Allowing our negative self to win the battle of "Should I or Shouldn't I", is a mistake. We need to go for it at every opportunity. We need to focus on our gifts and talents and not money, security, and employment. Don't just be a mediocre statistic, we need to love and live our career and grow, grow, grow!!!

Life is good!

Go, Go, Go…

Dan :)

Living Life on Life's Terms

"Never let life's hardships disturb you…no one can avoid problems, not even saints or sages."
– Nichiren Daishonin

Somehow early on in my life of recovery I began to think that if I were sober I somehow would avoid or totally eliminate problems in my life. I felt that if I was clean and sober the result should be total freedom from difficulty! As a matter of fact I used that presumption to relapse in the early years. I would blame my difficulties on God and say things like, "if this is what recovery is like I might as well be drunk"!

Of course I had no sponsor, I did no service work, I went to meetings on my own terms. I had no idea what mutual support or the steps were about. I thought I put the effort in, but in reality I was running the show and I was clueless!

True recovery is living life on life's terms. Recognizing that life is filled with challenges. Especially when we create challenges by our actions, which by the way I was extremely good at! Yet recovery allows us the opportunity to turn challenges into championships. To turn it all into something good!

Go, Go, Go...

Dan :)

Challenges

"Challenges make you discover things about yourself that you never really knew. They're what make the instrument stretch — what makes you go beyond the norm." – *Cicely Tyson*

I do not think there is any greater challenge that we face then the challenge of overcoming addiction for the addict. We learn through the recovery process that we are capable of much more than we ever imagined possible. We learn we can stretch further than we have ever. We become more flexible and prudent in our decision-making skills. We learn to strive for excellence yet we keep tabs by our progress and not a perception of perfection.

We begin to look to others for help and to help. We offer our love when in the past we looked for love. We develop friendship and camaraderie rather than a pretentious set of acquaintances and selfish reliance's on others. We become selfless rather than selfish. All through the great challenge of overcoming addiction and alcoholism! Life is good!!!

Go, Go, Go…

Dan :)

Resistance

You never change things by fighting the existing reality. To change something, build a new model that makes the existing model obsolete. *-- Richard Buckminster Fuller*

I do a quick exercise in my lectures I ask someone to put their hand up against mine. I put a little pressure on their hand with mine and they always push back. I have never had anyone not push back. Our nature is to push back. It is the same way with our mental status. As we add pressure our mind pushes back. To make effective change we must build a new model that we follow. We must realign our strategy and focus on that strategy rather than force change using the opposite of what we currently do.

Most of the people that I work with are successful in some area of their lives. I always point out to them that if they are successful in one area of life they can be successful in the other areas. Most folks attempting to recover from addiction fall victim to the three "P"s of helplessness.

Permanent; they believe their life condition is permanent.
Pervasive; that their condition pervades all areas of their lives.
Personal; where there is something wrong with them.

These are myths, if we simply change our strategy and focus on where we want to and are now heading, we will recover. For permanent sobriety and abstinence we must do the work so we clear out all the dirty laundry but primarily where our focus goes, energy flows!

Go, Go, Go...

Dan :)

Cherokee Rite of Passage

Do you know the legend of the Cherokee Indian youth's rite of Passage?

His father takes him into the forest, blindfolds him and leaves him alone.

He is required to sit on a stump the whole night and not remove the blindfold until the rays of the morning sun shine through it. He cannot cry out for help to anyone.

Once he survives the night, he is a MAN. He cannot tell the other boys of this experience, because each lad must come into manhood on his own. The boy is naturally terrified. He can hear all kinds of noises. Wild beasts must surely be all around him. Maybe even some human might do him harm. The wind blew the grass and earth, and shook his stump, but he sat stoically, never removing the blindfold. It would be the only way he could become a man!

Finally, after a horrific night the sun appeared and he removed his blindfold. It was then that he discovered his father sitting on the stump next to him... He had been at watch the entire night, protecting his son from harm. We, too, are never alone. Even when we don't know it, God is watching over us, sitting on the stump beside us. When trouble comes, All we have to do is reach out to Him.

Moral of the story: Just because you can't see God, Doesn't mean He is not there. 'For we walk by faith, not by sight.'

Breaking Down The Walls

"The individual is capable of both great compassion and great indifference. He has it within his means to nourish the former and outgrow the latter." – *Norman Cousins*

We are blessed to live a recovered life. Through the years and I will be honest enough to say in my personal life as well, I have seen many folks come in to the recovery process hardened. Guys or gals being released from prison, jails, or institutions attempting to use the tactics that kept them safe, come off as defiant or indifferent. Yet as time goes by in their recovery process the walls begin to shed and the freedom and love emerges. They begin to allow others to know and see that they feel, love and can love others for the first time in a very long time.

Greater yet is when we begin to move from indifference to compassion. When we start to do service work for others. When we see others hurting as we once hurt and we put a hand out to them. It is not by mistake that the field of human service is filled with people that were once on the other side of the coin. People that needed help are now helping others. Life is good!

Go, Go, Go...

Dan :)

We Are Meant To Be Somebody

"Life is not easy for any of us. But what of that? We must have perseverance and above all confidence in ourselves. We must believe that we are gifted for something and that this thing must be attained."
– Marie Curie

There are no two ways about it, we are meant to be somebody and do something special in and with our lives. That something is different for all of us. If we fail to live our lives with the passion we are blessed with we will meet each challenge we face with fear and worry. It is when we are utilizing our gifts for the good of others and fulfilling our destiny we discover that every challenge is a new opportunity to get better and better and better.

Life is good!

Go, Go, Go…

Dan :)

Contradictions

Contradiction is not a sign of falsity, nor the lack of contradiction a sign of truth. -- *Blaise Pascal*

The idea of alcoholism and addiction as a disease plays havoc in many peoples minds including the professionals. This concept has long been the center of debate for addiction and alcoholism researchers. For the addict it is a double-edged sword. Early on they fight the idea of an incurable disease and then often in treatment and for many in recovery they utilize it to escape responsibility for their actions or outcomes of their lives. Often people confuse commercial opinion for scientific or scholarly research. Lets face it authors claiming addiction is not a disease and can be cured are claims that can be directly related to personal or corporate monetary gain.

The question is does this make them wrong? Are the researchers wrong? How do we make sense of it all? In evaluation there are a number of contradictions in the disease concept or definitions.

The first thing we need to do is recognize that our human nature is to look for answers. Our minds need to make sense of everything. Chaos or disorder creates fear and panic in our lives, therefore our brains search for meaning. The harm in this debate has a lose-lose outcome. The truth is that alcoholism and/or addiction on the personal level are filled with perceived contradictions. The afflicted often look at their lives and situations and compare their plight to others around them in similar situations. In other words they look at others in treatment and proclaim they are not like that!

The second issue is "crackpot functionalism" that surrounds the malady. I cringe every time I listen to a recovering addict proclaim that their "alcoholism" has taken hold of them. They say things like, "my addiction is flaring up"! Talk about lack of responsibility! We use the disease concept to excuse our behaviors adding fuel to the fire.

What is right or wrong?

The first thing we must come to terms with is that there is no right or wrong in the disease debate when it comes to recovery. What matters is the end result. The twelve step experts claim that admission of powerlessness is essential to recover. What if this is simply semantics? What if an individual recognizes that alcohol or a drug (s) play a negative role in their lives and they choose to live abstinent? Is this a possibility? If alcoholism is progressive where does the progression begin? Can an individual change prior to crossing the line of addiction? Can the warning signs be heeded prior to full-blown alcohol dependence or addiction? What do you think?

Go, Go, Go...

Dan :)

A Set Back Is Just A Set Up For A Come Back!

"Let us endeavor so to live that when we come to die even the undertaker will be sorry." -- *Mark Twain*

A set back is just a set up for a come back! When we were young we had dreams of magnificence. If you hear of a young person losing their life to a tragic disease or accident of some sort, sadness will often come over you. If that child is part of your family you are devastated.

Many of us do not think of the ramifications of addiction in our lives. If we are active in our addiction and die, the story is sad. The funeral home is a sad place filled with stories of potential not met. But addiction is not the end for many of us. Recovery offers us a second chance at life. It is a set up for a come back.

We must live every day to the fullest, being the best that we can be. Developing into the human being that we were meant to be. Let the talk be at your funeral that of sadness but that of success. Do not leave us without your contribution being felt!

Go, Go, Go…

Dan :)

The Big Kid

"That's the real trouble with the world, too many people grow up. They forget. They don't remember what it's like to be twelve years old." — *Walt Disney*

I was told recently that I am a big kid! lol... I am a big kid, maturing and being a kid at heart is very different. I am a mature big kid! I love life and I am not afraid to let you know that. I have had some crazy challenges in my life and more specifically my recovered life. Most of them are of my own doing.

Last night I was working with my buddy "Sarge" with a group of folks it was the quintessential mature kid stuff! We laughed and joked and anchored home the reality of recovery. Our spiritual condition is serious yet joyful! I love life, I can attest to the fact the Sarge loves life and these group of folks are learning to love life! Life is meant to be enjoyed!!!

Go, Go, Go...

Dan :)

The How

"Once the 'what' is decided, the 'how' always follows. We must not make the 'how' an excuse for not facing and accepting the 'what.'" – *Pearl S. Buck*

We are blessed to have twelve-step programs and other mutual support recovery groups. The HOW is outlined for us. Tony Robbins once said, "Success leaves clues". Nowhere else can you find a greater example of this then in the rooms of twelve-step and other recovery groups. Rarely have we seen a person fail who has thoroughly followed our paths. This has proven to be factual for me over the years. The folks that make it are the ones that do what we have done. Those that do not make it are the ones that buck the system. Of course there are those less fortunate that are constitutionally incapable of being honest with themselves, however, I have found throughout the years they are few and far between.

If you want what we have and are willing to go to any lengths to achieve it, you will achieve sobriety. This is not theory this is reality, this is factual. Are there challenges in some of the AA, NA or other support groups? Certainly! In fact I have witnessed some stuff that I simply shake my head at in disbelief! Some of us get overly zealous and shift from suggesting to directing. However, if you want what we have, do what we do. The great thing about the recovery community is there are tons of meetings every day, you can find forums online, chat rooms, hotlines, and you can find other recovery programs, like SMART Recovery. If you are sick and tired of being sick and tired then do something different!

Go, Go, Go...

Dan :)

To Live

"To live is the rarest thing in the world. Most people exist, that is all." — *Oscar Wilde*

Living life to the fullest is so important especially for folks recovering from addiction. We do not get sober to merely exist; our second chance in life comes with a price. The price is to simply take life seriously! We need to live our lives like we mean it. This morning I came in to my office to a thank you card. It said, "I feel so empowered in life. I'm just going for it; I live by the ABC's. I love it. I'm so turned on by the way I think and behave. You tapped into a part of me that needed improvement. I always had it but I needed help."

I get excited for people when they recognize their power to change, to be all that they can be, to do all that their God given talents offer! Of course it goes without saying that I take zero credit for this, I am the messenger. But the point is life is meant to be enjoyed and not to be endured. Life is enjoyable when we live with purpose and passion!

Go, Go, Go...

Dan :)

EnthUUUsiasm

Every great and commanding movement in the annals of the world is due to the triumph of enthusiasm. Nothing great was ever achieved without it. -- *Ralph Waldo Emerson*

My friend Jimmy Meyer taught me one of my affirmations that I use every morning as part of my "Morning Mental Workout". Today I will win--- Why? I'll tell you why: Because I have faith, courage and EnthUUUUsiasm!!!

Enthusiasm, God Within!

If you get to know me personally you will recognize that I am motivated to help others to become all they can be. I am excited about life and love life, others and the journey. It is not me or my nature, in fact I was raised negatively. The truth is simple, if I did not get sober, allow God to guide my path and practice the principles I have been taught I would not have "Enthusiasm"!

I had difficulty on and off for many years with defining God in my life. Until I began to realize that God is within. That God is Love! Make today a great day filled with "Enthusiasm"!!!

Go, Go, Go...

Dan :)

More on Enthusiasm

Enthusiasm is one of the most powerful engines of success. When you do a thing, do it with all your might. Put your whole soul into it. Stamp it with your own personality. Be active, be energetic and faithful, and you will accomplish your object. Nothing great was ever achieved without enthusiasm.
-- Ralph Waldo Emerson

The word enthusiasm continues to come up in my life. It reminds me to keep my focus where it is needed, on God. Although I believe that God is always with me and within, when my focus is on living with purpose my life flows. When I am living selfishly or in greed my life garners turmoil and dissent. Keeping my mind fixed on the target, asking God to guide my path and remaining humble is the key for peace and serenity in my life.

When I live with enthusiasm things get accomplished in my life. I walk a bit differently, I talk a bit differently, I act and take action. It is that extra degree needed to get the water boiling. I believe that God wants each and every one of us to live to our fullest potential, to live with enthuuuuuuuusiasm!

Go, Go, Go...

Dan :)

Failure isn't Fatal

"You may have a fresh start any moment you choose, for this thing that we call 'failure' is not the falling down, but the staying down." -- *Mary Pickford*

Most of us look at failure the wrong way. To be honest it truly stinks to fail, trust me I have done enough failing for all of us. Especially when I fail due to my own poor choices or my actions are not intense enough to cause the blisters! Failure is not fatal, yet it does feel that way.

Some years ago someone made the observation that relapse is part of recovery. Well of course that is a half-truth. For some folks they do relapse, in fact for this guy my first attempt at recovery lead me on an eight-year journey of ups and downs. My goal was not to remain abstinent, my goal was to stop the hurting, stay out of prison, keep my family from driving me crazy and other reasons. I absolutely count that as part of my recovery history. However, the truth is I did not commit to abstinence or recovery.

The greatest challenge we face with this thought process is it puts a reservation in the back of our heads. The truth is we can fail in life, we can make mistakes in our recovery and we do not need to relapse. We must stop telling ourselves that any failure is fatal. If we make a mistake we need to get up, dust off, admit the challenge, amend the action, and learn from it. Drinking or drugging will only make it worse!

Go, Go, Go...

Dan :)

Growing Up

"If we don't change, we don't grow. If we don't grow, we are not really living. Growth demands a temporary surrender of security." – *Gail Sheehy*

Growing up is part of recovery. They say that when we began to drink and/or drug we stopped growing emotionally. We need to pick up where we left off or were left off. Chronologically we are one age but emotionally we are much younger.

In order to grow we must change, we must take risks even risks that are extremely calculated. I recognize that not everyone has the personality to be a risk taker, however there are risks that we must take if we expect to be successful in recovery. For instance, there is an important risk we should take, i.e. "the risk of asking someone to be our sponsor or mentor".

If we want joy in our life we must grow up. If we want peace in our life we must change the way we see things, respond to life events and take the necessary risks when faced with change! Life is good!

Go, Go, Go...

Dan :)

Forgiveness

"Forgiveness is the economy of the heart....forgiveness saves the expense of anger, the cost of hatred, the waste of spirits." – *Hannah More*

Forgiveness starts with **ME** 100% of the time. The spiritual axiom that when I am frustrated, angry, jealous, or any other emotion of negativity I must look at myself first. I must search for the cause within myself. Typically forgiveness is a two way street. They say it takes two to tango! But it always starts with **ME!**

My relationship with people depends upon my ability to see clearly my actions and how they inter-relate with others. How I perceive any situation or inter-communication must start with self-examination. Restraint of tongue and pen is essential if I am to have inner peace and joy. Lashing out creates anxiety, confusion and distorts the messages that I am attempting to express.

Life is way too good to screw it up because my ego says I am right and they are wrong! I need to look and keep my side of the street clean in all I do. Then and only then can I forgive or be forgiven!

Go, Go, Go...

Dan :)

Change is Inevitable

"We must dare to think "unthinkable" thoughts. We must learn to explore all the options and possibilities that confront us in a complex and rapidly changing world." – *James William Fulbright*

Change is inevitable. We are all changing on a daily basis. The world changes around us whether we like it or not. In order to live happy, joyous and free we must change our negative patterns with positive disciplines. In order for us to excel in our lives we must stretch ourselves and remold ourselves into positive, vibrant, and productive people. We must utilize our God given talent to the fullest.

If your goals and dreams do not seem impossible they are probably not going to stretch you enough. The more we explore the impossible the greater our potential becomes. The greater our potential becomes the greater life gets! Life is good!

Go, Go, Go…

Dan :)

Pushing Others Up

"The more credit you give away, the more will come back to you. The more you help others, the more they will want to help you." - *Brian Tracy*

Pushing others up, offering people a pat on the back for a job well done can be the difference for them in their recovery. The founders of AA knew something about people when they wrote the twelve-steps. Offer suggestions, lead the way and encourage others by helping them when needed, all with no expectation of reward or gain.

The more we help others get what they want, the more we get what we want. What is it that we all want? JOY, we all want joy in our lives. We want to be happy, joyous and free. It is simple, do for others and joy will abound in you!

Go, Go, Go…

Dan :)

Gratitude Is Key To Happiness And Joy

"As soon as you start to feel differently about what you already have, you will start to attract more of the good things, more of the things you can be grateful for." — *Joe Vitale*

Gratitude is key to happiness and joy. Having an attitude of gratitude helps to keep us focused on the main thing, living one day at a time focused on our purpose. When we have a grateful heart we are positive, upbeat, fulfilled, vibrant, alive and ready to tackle any task placed in our path!

Early on in the recovery process people struggle to find things to be truly grateful for. I always suggest that they use the A to Z method so they search deep for answers. Starting with the letter A what am I grateful for? For me it is my Aunt Maureen, she always made me feel special...

I have been blessed to see people that take the exercise seriously grow in gratitude and understanding that everything has a purpose, which as Joe Vitale says in his best selling book "The Attractor Factor", "Turn It Into Something Good"!

Today, let's turn it all into something good!

Go, Go, Go...

Dan :)

DO IT!

"Great things are done by a series of small things brought together."
— *Vincent van Gogh*

One day at a time, step-by-step, and easy does it, but DO IT! There are periods of time that I look back at and realize how I allowed frustration to set in. I wanted it all and I wanted it now. I was willing to pay the price but I wanted to be sober, done with drama in life, financially secure and living in abundance immediately. I remember seeing guys and gals come into the rooms and within ninety days have their family back, their careers on overdrive and expressing their joy and happiness about how good their life has become. I remember being frustrated that I was sober a year and I seemed to continue to struggle in these areas.

Yet the intestinal fortitude and the ability to not quit no matter what happened paid off. I learned how to think well. I learned how to be in alignment rather than fighting. Slowly the little things began and continued to pay off. Today I look back with an eye of gratitude that I kept moving forward and did not allow my stinking thinking to get the best of me!

Go, Go, Go…

Dan :)

Guilt and Shame are BS

"The most important thing is to be whatever you are without shame."
- Rod Steiger

Guilt and shame are emotions we cannot afford to accommodate on a daily basis. I have often heard it said that guilt is a BS emotion. Of course that is not completely true, it is definitely an emotion that we need to experience it keeps us honest. However, it is when we utilize the emotion to beat ourselves up that it is toxic and counterproductive. Many of us use guilt and shame to stay sick. We use it to pity ourselves and remain stuck in the problem rather than focus on the solution.

The twelve-step process guides us in overcoming these anchors that baffle us. When we get serious about recovery and we do the work we are no longer afflicted with the negative blame game thoughts. We begin to live happy, joyous and free. We live with passion and purpose and we tackle the emotions before they become toxic! Life is good!

Go, Go, Go…

Dan :)

We Are Born To Be Dreamers

"First comes thought; then organization of that thought, into ideas and plans; then transformation of those plans into reality. The beginning, as you will observe, is in your imagination." — *Napoleon Hill*

We are born to be dreamers. We start out believing we can do anything! Yet as time goes by we start to believe there are limits to our dreams. As we grow we begin to get the "reality" messages from our family, friends, teachers, and other important folks that help shape our belief system. If we are from an alcoholic, addicted or other significant dysfunction within our family it is even more likely that we start to believe the message that we are limited.

As we shape our recovery we must keep in mind that we can be, do and have what we want. We no longer are limited to average and ordinary. One word of caution is we need to keep our priorities straight and not chase money or other things as the end. We must be purpose driven, living our lives with excitement and passion. Utilizing our talents and gifts to the max! Do not believe the lie that you are limited. Do not believe the lie that you are lucky to be sober and that you should be a good little soldier now. You are forgiven for your wrongs if you work the steps thoroughly; this is your chance to fulfill your destiny!

Go, Go, Go…

Dan :)

Live With Excitement

Enthusiasm is the most beautiful word in the world. - *Christian Morgenstern*

I would not classify myself as a linguist however I love words when I recognize their meaning and root. In this case according to Dictionary.com the root of the word enthusiasm, is Greek, énthous, variant of éntheos having a god within. The meaning of the word is; "absorbing the mind by any interest or pursuit, a lively interest". When we think of people that are enthusiastic we think of people that are excited, motivated and pumped up about their life. They live with passion!

In recovery we gain a new life, we live with excitement and passion for the renewed spirit. We trust in God and are grateful for the second chance. Life gets better and better and better as we grow through the principles of recovery.

For me personally, I awaken every day motivated to enjoy the day and be productive! When my eyes open I thank God for a new day, I remind myself that I am alive, awake and feel great! I read and say my affirmations every day, my favorite affirmation is:

My attitude everyday will determine my success in the future. Today I will walk, talk, act and believe like the person I wish to become!!!

I deserve success & will do what successful people do. I refuse to allow negative people to fill my mind with negativity!!!

Most of the arguments I have are with myself. So when I get down I will use the famous GOYA (get off your anatomy) formula for guaranteed success!!!

Today I will win --- Why? I'll tell you why: Because I have faith, courage and EnthUUUUsiasm!!!

Go, Go, Go…

Dan :)

Opportunity to Grow

Victims are victimized. *--Jack Jackson*

When things go wrong and they do, we have a tendency to look for the why. Often the why points to other people, places or conditions, rarely if ever back at us. Not only does it take us off the hook but it in some way feels better to blame someone else. To rant and rave about another human being and their ineptitude or stupidity that affected the outcome for us feels good or at best relieving. Can you spell victim? Yes the victim mentality is at work and winning!

The challenge with that line of thinking is you are probably wrong! More importantly at some level you actually know it and you roll with it anyway. There is no doubt however that this line of thinking is unhealthy to say the least. That is due in part that the role is self-limiting even self-destructive and pushes us into a self-perpetuating negative loop.

The loop goes like this, things don't go your way, so you get angry and blame someone else. But deep down you know that it is really your own fault, so you feel guilty, ashamed and begin to beat yourself up internally. Your self-confidence decreases and your doubt increases like a merry-go-round you spin!

To grow past this behavior we must begin to think of others first and ourselves last. A sense of humility and an attitude of service to others first is the way off the merry-go-round. When we put the needs of others ahead of our own we begin to relieve ourselves of the burden of self and we open our lives up to abounding joy.

Life is good!

Go, Go, Go…

Dan ☺

Rome Wasn't Built In A Day

"When you have a great and difficult task, something perhaps almost impossible, if you only work a little at a time, every day a little, suddenly the work will finish itself." – *Isak Dinesen*

Rome wasn't built in a day. Many of us in the early days of our recovery process are impossibly impatient. We want it all and we want it now. What I have learned over the course of time is work, works! Nothing good in this world comes for free. When we work at something the reward is that much better. I remember the 90 day wonders that would share how great life is for them and how they have gotten their lives back together. They had great jobs; their family was on their side, and other great things that worked to their benefit.

At the time I would think wow what about me? Why can't I find work? My family is in ruins, I don't have a car, and I am broke! It didn't take long to find out that most of those people disappeared. Things weren't as good as they made it out to sound. Over the years many of them have come back after years of use and abuse, none have reported that it got any better for them!

We need to be and stay patient, we need to do the work and live every day to the fullest.

Go, Go, Go...

Dan :)

Face Fear

"I have accepted fear as a part of life, specifically the fear of change, the fear of the unknown. I have gone ahead despite the pounding in the heart that says: Turn back, turn back; you'll die if you venture too far." – *Erica Jong*

We all face fear, an early acronym I remember being used when it came to fear was False Evidence Appearing Real. The truth is that we all feel fear it is a natural emotion; it is the "Fight or Flight" emotion. Without it we would probably not survive because we would put ourselves into serious risk in situations that could be fatal.

However, we must recognize that reacting to fear based upon strictly emotion is avoidable and not recommended. We must be cautious that we do not live only via emotion. Our emotions can and do play tricks on us. When we live in the emotion we have a tendency to be more reactive. When we live a balanced emotional life we tend to be more responsive. The difference can produce extremely opposite results. Life is way to good to waste on drama!

Go, Go, Go…

Dan :)

Action and Purpose

"Time is limited, so I better wake up every morning fresh and know that I have just one chance to live this particular day right, and to string my days together into a life of action, and purpose." -- *Lance Armstrong*

Action and purpose are the key ingredients to a happy, joyous and free life. Of course for the addict abstinence is essential and the main thing! Recently I was reading a research study on the key aspects of people with long-term sobriety in mutual support groups. The study indicated two pertinent features or variables that people with long-term sobriety had or followed.

1) Sponsor, people that have attained prolonged recovery had and used a sponsor. This makes quite a bit of sense to me; even professional athletes have and use coaches.

2) Service, people that get and stay sober perform service within their mutual support groups. What is service? In terms of life it is the fulfillment of our purpose, it is living a life of purpose! In action: Helping others to help themselves.

It is a given that people that have a sponsor and perform service attend meetings. What are meetings? ACTION! What is service ACTION and PURPOSE! Live passionately and live life well! You deserve it!

Go, Go, Go...

Dan :)

The Connection

"The tragedy in life doesn't lie in not reaching your goal. The tragedy lies in having no goal to reach."
– Benjamin Mays

I have a busy week that started for me on Friday. I went to visit my cousin Bill and his wife Beth in Northern Florida. I drove back on Saturday night and then over to visit my cousin Stephanie in Fort Myers on Sunday for lunch. Swung down to pick up my son Sean and headed back to Fort Lauderdale where my sons Liam and Seamus came in for spring break from New York. I am excited to have a week of fun in the sun with my three sons. We are going to a Miami Heat game, Billy Swamp Safari and South Beach.

On Friday and Saturday with Bill and Beth we had a ball. I have always looked up to my cousin Bill and loved his dad my Uncle Harry. We had the chance to reminisce about our time with Uncle Harry in fact one of his favorite sayings was "youth is wasted on the young". I know what he means today I didn't as a teen! Bill is sober as well so it makes for a great visit we went to his home group Saturday morning early to help set up. It was the anniversary of the group 26 years as a group and best of all it was an "Eating Meeting"! I had the chance to indulge in some home made Raspberry French Toast and Bill well he tried everything from the buffet it was an amazing sight he never asked what anything was he just tried it! I am not there yet!

My trip to visit Stephanie was pleasant as well. I held out hope for Stephanie for years, while Bill is sober 24 years Stephanie has just started her recovery journey, 52 days. The amazing thing to me is the vigor she has for life now; she goes to meetings daily, has a sponsor does service work and attends IOP and individual therapy at the V.A.

As I write I cannot help to think that Bill a retiree sober 24 years has a vigor for life, he does service work he has a sponsor and an amazing support group and family. Stephanie just starting out does service work attends meetings, has a sponsor and an amazing support group of women on her side and you can see the life back in her eyes! I wonder if there is a connection? Boy, life is goooooood!!! Go, Go, Go...
Dan :)

Recovery Thinking, 90 Days to Change Your Life!

Living Your Life

Life is an Adventure! -- *Me*

Recovery is about Living Your Life to its Fullest! Through the years I have seen many people give up on life. They confuse living life on life's terms with settling for less then they are capable of. We are all here on this earth for a reason. We all have strengths and weaknesses. We all have the ability to be, do, and have anything we want.

As you probably know, the hit movie "The Secret" increased the world's awareness to the Law of Attraction, the principle that states that we are "responsible" for attracting to us everything that shows up in our lives. Now, we're not taking about responsible in terms of blame or fault. However, if we are not feeling successful, happy, at peace, abundant, in good health, and surrounded by fun and loving people, it would serve us to examine how we have attracted these situations to us.

So, the question remains, "Exactly HOW do we manifest those things we want most in our lives?" How do we attract wealth and abundance? How do we attract supportive, loving people? How do we achieve blissful happiness and peace of mind and live a relatively upset-free life?

I was interviewing a successful gentleman a number of years ago. I asked him, "what advice would you give to someone that is looking to achieve success in life"? He said, "find someone that knows where they are going, and has a plan to get there. Then unlatch your little red wagon from whatever you have it attached to and hook it onto that leader. Because no one does it alone"!

Tony Robbins says, "Success Leaves Clues". Find someone that has achieved the success you are looking for, do what he or she does and you will get what he or she has! The answer is simple although it is not easy. It takes work, commitment and it takes an experienced Mentor. Someone that knows what they are doing, where they are going, and knows how to help you to get to where you want to go. Life is good!

Go, Go, Go...

Dan ☺

Priorities

"Life is an opportunity, benefit from it.
Life is beauty, admire it.
Life is bliss, taste it.
 Life is a dream, realize it.
Life is a challenge, meet it.
Life is a duty, complete it.
Life is a game, play it.
Life is a promise, fulfill it.
Life is sorrow, overcome it.
Life is a song, sing it.
Life is a struggle, accept it.
Life is a tragedy, confront it.
Life is an adventure, dare it.
Life is luck, make it.
Life is too precious, do not destroy it.
Life is life, fight for it."
-- *Mother Teresa*

When my cousin Joey died at the age of 46, it was an absolute shock to me. It made me think about my priorities, challenges, struggles, and direction. I thought to myself in a very different way then ever before, "why would I worry or panic in any situation? I can only do what I can do here and now. The best practice for me is to work as hard as I can, love as much as I can, be the best person today and take everything else as it comes". Of course, I have heard those things said before and I have said them to alleviate the pressure. But now I was saying them with a twist, "today could be my last day on this earth!"

I recognize from a different perspective today that "Life is Good". Today I live with a true passion to be the Beacon of Hope for people that struggle with addiction. Recovery is about Life, it is as expressed by Mother Teresa an "Opportunity"!

There is a paradigm shift that must take place in all of us. That shift must entail Mother Teresa's Mantra. Regret for our past is a sin. Yes, regret for our past is a sin. It is hurtful and painful. It has no place in the recovered persons thoughts. The twelve steps are designed to eliminate regret so that an individual can live to their potential. Living to your potential takes guts. Living to your potential takes 100% responsibility for your life and your decisions. Conformity is dangerous. Abiding by the law of man is required however conforming to the mediocre mentality of others is dangerous. Life is good!

Go, Go, Go…

Dan ☺

Challenge Life

Living in the Day, it takes practice! – *Me again…*

When it comes to facing life's challenges folks in recovery are typically taught to live in the day. In other words we cannot overcome a major issue all at once. Take the time to evaluate the situation and not project what the outcome will be. In early recovery we tend to project the result as a negative outcome. Often these negative projections lead to "analysis paralysis". We freeze!

When we freeze it only hurts our progress. Typically, only negative results occur from this form of inaction. The key is not to lose control of your emotions, stay in the moment and in control when everything around you is out of control. You must focus on where you want to go and not on your fear.

How do you accomplish this? It takes practice start with the little things that come up. I was recently reminded of a technique to utilize when your car is out of control. It is strongly recommended to focus on where you want the car to head rather then on where you do not want the vehicle to end up. In other words focus on the open road and not the trees! This is exactly what we need to do in our lives. Focus on where we want to go in life rather than on where we do not want to go.

Focus equals Power, focus enough on what you want and you will condition yourself to steer out of the spin in total control.

Life is good!

Go, Go, Go…

Dan ☺

Love And Be Loved

"Love is what we are born with. Fear is what we have learned here. The spiritual journey is the unlearning of fear and the acceptance of love back into our hearts." — *Marianne Williamson*

When I think of fear I start with the idea that it is a natural occurrence, "fight or flight" is what comes to mind. But for those of us that have faced the demon of addiction fear is the over abundance of our negative self. We have developed an unhealthy dose of fear and we react to it as if it is a reality. We drink and drug due to its effects on us. We ruin relationships because of it.

Spirituality shows us how to love and to be loved. I remember early in my recovery being told that people would love me back to health. I grasped onto that with a vengeance. I wanted to be loved more than anything else in this world. Today I see fear for what it is and I have love and joy in my heart. It all starts with letting others in and accepting that love as reality over fear!

Go, Go, Go...

Dan :)

Beyond Gratitude

This is a note I received on Facebook.

"Hi, just thought i would let you know I have not touched a drop for 9 months now :) the emails I get from your website help loads, love reading them. My kids are now very happy to have their mum back, has been bloody hard at times but the closer it gets to a year the more determined I am....... xx"

On Friday I received a call from my oldest son Sean. We were set to have dinner that night. He said, "hey dad I was invited to a football combine for the CFL, UFL and AFL. It is up in Jacksonville tomorrow will you go with me?" Of course I said yes, I was already on my way to his house for a planned visit so I turned around and grabbed some clothes for an overnight trip.

Tears in my eyes I thanked God for another day in recovery. I know that as a drunk I was unpredictable and could not be relied upon. On the five-hour trip he thanked me a few times for going with him! Yet it was an honor and a pleasure for me to be going! When I get messages like above I am happy that I can share my recovery with others. Yet selfishly it is times like Friday I am grateful that I stayed the course and remained sober one day at a time. Life is GOOOOOOOD!!!

Go, Go, Go…

Dan :)

The Price Tag

"Only a man who knows what it is like to be defeated can reach down to the bottom of his soul and come up with the extra ounce of power it takes to win when the match is even." – *Muhammad Ali*

Recovery comes with a price tag. The price is the willingness to give back what we have been freely given. As a survivor and overcomer we know what it is like to reach down through the fear and recover. Addiction is no match for those of us that have recovered. We know what it takes to win we can reach down for that extra ounce of power, the power within, our spiritual guide and force.

Because we know what it was like, what we did to face the demons and what it is like now we can help others do the same. Our lives have become manageable, God has done for us what we could not have done for ourselves and today we give to those that need that guidance. Bill and Bob recognized something that no one before them knew, service to the still sick and suffering alcoholic and addict is essential. Service is the price, a small price for the return! Life is good!!!

Go, Go, Go…

Dan :)

Mutual Support

Coming together is a beginning, staying together is progress, and working together is success. *- Henry Ford*

There is magic in mutual support groups. Coming together to share our experience, strength and hope allows an individual to grow beyond their wildest dreams. Today it is amazing to see people come as they are and become whom they ARE within. Early on they believe the lie that they are what they have done. They focus on the wrong they have done and consider that, who they are. Wrong, wrong, wrong!!! That is not who you are that is what you have done!

Over the years I have noticed that many people beginning the recovery process think they are "bad people", but the truth is, most people are good at heart. Most people want to be something they can be proud of. Most people want to win in life. The magic of mutual support is that over time people see that they truly are winners, they are good and they love and are loved!

Go, Go, Go…

Dan :)

Never Give Up

Other people and things can stop you temporarily. You're the only one who can do it permanently.
-- Zig Ziglar

I have a quote on my desk by Sir Winston Churchill that reminds me to never give up, never, never, never... Winning in life is an inside job. We must be willing to face the fear, negativity and our own doubt. But we cannot allow any of that to stop us from achieving our purpose here on earth.

Those of us that have recovered from this dreadful disease of addiction and those of us in the process know the depths of despair that addiction and alcoholism has taken us. Today we have the hope for a prosperous future a rewarding future filled with happiness and joy, but we must stay focused on the rewards and keep doing the work no matter what we are told or think. We cannot afford to allow negativity to rear its ugly head in our path.

I have been blessed to work with individuals on a daily basis that are new to the recovery process and when I see the hope in their eyes for the first time in many years it gets me excited. Life is meant to be enjoyed and not endured and when we succumb to the negativity we endure life! So never, ever, ever quit on yourself, never!

Go, Go, Go...

Dan :)

No Regret, another view…

Never regret. If it's good, it's wonderful. If it's bad, it's experience. -- *Victoria Holt*

Regret is a terrible thing we all make mistakes if we learn from the mistakes we move on. We can't we live in regret. That is correct, many people think that learning from mistakes means that we never make the same mistake. That is total BS right there and I don't care who you are. We all make the same mistake more than once. We all make similar mistakes the concept is a good one but it is simply not valid.

The danger in making the same mistake over and over again is that we get numb to the consequences. When we get numb to the consequences we have moved into a negative way of living, this is contrary to sober living. When we feel the pain, make adjustments and work towards making amends for our actions we are living in the recovery process. The truth of the matter is this, we did not get this way overnight and we will not recover overnight either. Recovery is a process, a lifelong process! But it is worth it! Life is good!

Go, Go, Go…

Dan :)

Goals

You are never too old to set another goal or to dream a new dream. --
C.S. Lewis

My friend and mentor Jack Jackson is 81 years old, sober 50 years and
continues to set goals. He believes that as long as he is here on earth he
will enjoy life. He believes that when your life is completed you will take
your last breath. Jack is a Jacob Marino proponent. It is reported that
Jacob the night before he passed away went to bed and said my life has
been a great life and I have fulfilled my potential here, I am done,
goodbye. Then he closed his eyes, went to sleep and died. Jack's mantra
is simple, "Life is meant to be enjoyed and not to be endured".

Yesterday I met with a gentleman in early recovery. He is 50 years old
and he said he met a few men that were in their seventies and sober 20
plus years. He said that it gave him hope. He felt that at 50 years old he
felt that he had nothing to look forward to. He thought he was too old to
recover. But now that he met these other men he has hope. We are never
too old to get sober and fulfill our lives.

I remember when I got sober there was a fellow his name was Charlie he
was in his seventies as well. But Charlie was beginning the recovery
process. Charlie had lost his wife and fell into a drunken existence. I
remember when I first met him I thought, "what is this guy doing? He is
so old! In fact he had no teeth and could not walk without a walker and
assistance. A month after I celebrated my first recovery anniversary so
did Charlie. Charlie lived out his life sober, productive and contributing to
life! Life is good!!!!!!

Go, Go, Go…

Dan :)

Psychic Change

On the other hand—and strange as this may seem to those who do not understand—once a psychic change has occurred, the very same person who seemed doomed, who had so many problems he despaired of ever solving them, suddenly finds himself easily able to control his desire for alcohol, the only effort necessary being that required to follow a few simple rules. *—Alcoholics Anonymous, 4th ed., pg. xxix*

Those who cannot are those that will not… a few simple adjustments in life can and will free us from addiction. In the addiction treatment realm of the world we see so many folks failing to remain clean and sober. Yet when the curtain is pushed aside it simply comes down to one thing, does the person want to get well?

I am not a huge spy on Facebook but it amazes me that people that say they want to get and stay sober continue on with their old behaviors. Glorifying addiction and the negative behaviors of addiction are counter-productive. Folks living in halfway houses that break the rules are not necessarily heading in the right direction. Recovery takes following a few simple suggestions, patience, diligence, commitment, and a desire to stop using.

Give yourself a shot at life, say yes to life, if you think you know better, remember this simple rule of thumb, "YOU DON'T". Life is way too good to waste, go seize the day!

Go, Go, Go…

Dan :)

Why Worry?

Why worry? We lose way too much energy when we worry. Worry often brings fear and fear paralyzes most of us. The truth is that most of what we worry about never occurs. Try this on for size, what were you worried about on March 22, 2010? How about the month of March in 2010? How about March 3 of this year? Ask yourself, "did the issue I was worried about come to pass"? If not, why? If so, "was it as devastating as I thought"? Approximately 8% of what we worry about actually comes to pass. Worry only makes it worse.

Face Fear with Passion and Belief! Believe that all things work out for the good. Believe that if you continue to take the right actions the right things will happen. Believe that if it is going to be it is up to me! Say YES to life and make it happen!

Go, Go, Go…

Dan :)

Excellence

If you are going to achieve excellence in big things, you develop the habit in little matters. Excellence is not an exception, it is a prevailing attitude. *--Colin Powell*

When I think of excellence I think back to my propensity to judge myself radically. In the early years of recovery I would get down on my mistakes and myself. Fortunately for the fellowship and my support group it was pointed out to me that we strive for spiritual progress not spiritual perfection. Over the years I have learned there is a difference between perfection and excellence.

Perfection is the need to be right while excellence is the drive to take action. When we act with the tools we have been given, developed and taught we are living in excellence. We strive to do what is right, rewarding and beneficial to others and us. Excellence is always in the actions.

Go, Go, Go…

Dan ☺

Priorities

The key is not to prioritize what's on your schedule, but to schedule your priorities. *-- Stephen R. Covey*

In early recovery one thing some folk's worry about is "how am I going to get to meetings for 90 straight days"? Often that question is not about the time it is more about the priority level. There are several priority issues an individual questions when faced with this aspect of recovery.

There is family time, work, recreation, socialization and other challenges such as educational pursuits to name a few of the important ones. These are all extremely valid issues and considerations however many of us have no balance in our lives prior to recovery either. The binge drinker that stops for one drink and never leaves the tavern does not fulfill their responsibility to their family. Therefore a ninety-day immersion into a new way of life is a small price to pay. A price that any family member will vote YES for if asked for their blessing!

As we begin to recover and move through the steps a healthy balance between all priorities is necessary to live happy, joyous and free. Having a schedule written down, preferably in a calendar or if you are like most folks today in your smart phone calendar with an alarm reminder for the important stuff will help you balance your time and priorities.   If you want what we have, do what we do!

Go, Go, Go...

Dan :)

The Essentials: GOALS

"The greater danger for most of us lies not in setting our aim too high and falling short; but in setting our aim too low, and achieving our mark." – *Michelangelo Buonarroti*

Setting goals is essential in life. We are here for a flicker. Too many of us settle for mediocre lives. I could quote Henry David Thoreau all day on this topic but this comes to mind; "If one advances confidently in the direction of his dreams, and endeavors to live the life which he has imagined, he will meet with a success unexpected in common hours".

We need hope to recover, I believe we must love and be loved as well. I remember in "The Strangest Secret" Earl Nightingale states that out of 100 people at the age of 65 only 5 have achieved their dreams, the rest are still working, indigent, and often miserable. For the alcoholic or addict this is dangerous.

I am not talking strictly financial if you have listened to the audio you know that success is doing the thing you love and doing it well. Wealth does not define our lives purpose defines our lives. In the beginning we suggest to the unemployed or the directionless individual to go get a sobriety job. Get something that you can do that will bring in cash to meet your basic needs. But, never take your eye off the mark, recovery, abstinence, direction and purpose!

Go, Go, Go...

Dan :)

Don't Quit Before The Miracle

Most people give up just when they're about to achieve success. They quit on the one yard line. They give up at the last minute of the game one foot from a winning touchdown. *-- Ross Perot*

I have heard it said many times in the rooms, "don't quit before the miracle happens". I took that advice to heart and have learned that it is never over there is always over time. When the times seem bleak and it looks like there is nowhere to turn stay focused because better times are ahead.

As much as I know it is not about willpower it is more about higher power sometimes we just gotta hang on tight. Don't drink and go to meetings takes on a life of its own. Don't drink even if your ass falls off is more like it. Happy, Joyous and Free comes for those that want it and work for it. If you quit joy will elude you...

Go, Go, Go...

Dan :)

Celebrate

"I think the purpose of life is to be useful, to be responsible, to be honorable, to be compassionate. It is, after all, to matter: to count, to stand for something, to have made some difference that you lived at all."
– Leo Rosten

Each year on April 14th I celebrate my recovery birthday or anniversary. My first year I was happy about the accomplishment but, I felt I was celebrating something that I should have been doing anyway, living clean, sober and productive! Then year two came and I was very prideful of the fete. In year three I remember the old timers at my group would fly back from Florida to celebrate. They would talk and talk and talk and the meeting would go on for nearly two hours. I would think man this is not about them. This is to show that it works! I was a bit pompous I guess.

Today I have the belief, that I share the day with every newcomer to say hey this works and it works well! Today I do not have an opinion on why others celebrate or how long they share. It is how they feel. It is something to be proud of! For me I believe Leo Rosten, the purpose of life is to be useful to others!

The morning of my 23rd anniversary the first e-mail I read came from my son Sean. It said congrats, lets do dinner, and I made something for you for your anniversary. If I could share the rewards that I have received through the years it would be a two-hour read! What drives me today is the desire to make a difference in peoples lives, including my families! Life is good!!!!

Go, Go, Go…

Dan :)

God who?

Faith without doubt is not faith! -- *Joe O'Sullivan*

For many years I struggled with my spirituality. I was a victim so I blamed God for my troubles. Then when I was told to go to God for help it freaked me out! My sponsor was an Irish Christian Brother and I remember one day I told him that I was having trouble with my concept of God, I could not believe the chair, or the clock, or any object could be my higher power as I had heard others say in the rooms. It was more difficult for me to believe that there was no God then to believe there is God. I simply couldn't fathom the theory that the world began and rushed endlessly nowhere.

I had such deep thoughts! As I was attempting to express this to him he quickly looked me in the eye and said, "knock it off Danny, you know there is a God and who God is"! I never forgot that event. When I begin to doubt I think about that quick conversation. I also remember my second sponsor telling me the "faith without doubt is not faith"! Today there are times that I question my belief and my motive, but I always come back to those two pearls!

Go, Go, Go...

Dan :)

What People Really Want from a Sponsor

The greatest deception men suffer is from their own opinions. -- *Leonardo Da Vinci*

What people really want from a sponsor is to have one. Most people in the early part of recovery have no idea why they need a supportive sponsor or the role of a sponsor. A sponsor is a guy or gal that helps introduce the newcomer to AA, NA or any of the other mutual support groups that are twelve step based in the early phase of recovery. A sponsor is a mentor, an individual that has overcome alcohol and/or drug addiction that will share with you their experience strength and hope.

It is not limited to early recovery. Typically, a member will have a sponsor that becomes a true friend someone that can help a recovering person get through the ups and downs of life, however that is not always the case. They are people that have recovered using the twelve steps and offer the same guidance they received from the folks that came before them.

A sponsor does not tell you what to do, they are not a parent, spouse or therapist. They simply guide you through the principles and steps of the program. They do not imply that they are smarter than you or know what you should do in any given situation. They will offer their experience and share with you what they have done to overcome similar issues.

If you are serious about your recovery find a sponsor and use him or her and remember men with the men and women with the women! Life is good!

Go, Go, Go...

Dan :)

What If?

"You may never know what results come from your action. But if you do nothing, there will be no result." – *Mahatma Gandhi*

The big what if!!! What if I would have? What if I fail? What if it is wrong for me? There are far too many what If's in life to name them all. The bottom line is that we will never know what if…! If we don't start somewhere. We all know what it is like to start if we are in the recovery process. That is the big start! Yet there is so much more to do in our lives. We are not here to simply stay sober. We are given a great opportunity to utilize our God given talents, a second chance at life!

Andrew Carnegie was recorded as saying that we all have two major opportunities in life. The question I have for you is, "Is this YOUR first or YOUR last"? Truthfully we simply don't know so do not take it lightly! Begin by changing your attitude, we all start with a fairly negative attitude, begin to change yours to a positive slant. Follow your ABC's and live strong, cause life is good!

A. Always be positive…
B. Be a student of life…
C. Cheerlead others…

Go, Go, Go…

Dan :)

Do It Till You Love It!

"Iron rusts from disuse; stagnant water loses its purity and in cold weather becomes frozen; even so does inaction sap the vigor of the mind." -- Leonardo da Vinci

I am never amazed when I hear the question, "do I have to do this forever"? or the statement, "I am not going to meetings forever"! The truth is, over the course of time we change and we find out that our recovered life takes effort, this is not exclusive to recovery. People that are happy, joyous and free whether in recovery or not, stay active in their lives. They live their lives with PURPOSE. They get up in the morning grateful for another day and they hit the pillow at night grateful for another successful day on earth.

Living a life of purpose gives us something to wake up to and the hope to awaken in the morning. To me this is relapse prevention. Stay active in your life, give to others, and be grateful!

Go, Go, Go...

Dan :)

Inch by Inch

"We do not have to become heroes overnight. Just a step at a time, meeting each thing that comes up, seeing it is not as dreadful as it appeared, discovering we have the strength to stare it down." -- *Eleanor Roosevelt*

Inch by inch it's a cinch, yard by yard it's hard… Many times in recovery we want it all and we want it all right now! But the truth is that we grow over time. We strengthen our resolve day by day. As we grow so does our commitment to recover. We strengthen our commitment to live abstinent lives. If we are confronted with a choice to "use" or "drink" we recognize how powerless "it" is over us! We have the strength to stay the course, to live happy, joyous and free! We recognize that God is doing for us what we cannot do ourselves. Life is good!

Go, Go, Go…

Dan :)

Great Opportunities

"The great secret of success in life is for a man to be ready when his opportunity comes." — *Benjamin Disraeli*

When we join the land of the living and stop living a life in the death race we are opened up to growth opportunities galore. We begin to see the light of day and we have the opportunity to choose success. The truth is that success is not an accident. Success comes to those that put the footwork into the process.

When we open up our minds to live a successful life, we no longer consider self-sabotage. We begin to choose life and life more abundantly. We start out our day in prayer and meditation choosing to do God's will in our journey. We ask what do you want me to do today? Who do you want me to bless today? How can I be of service to others? When we live the recovered life success attracts success…

Go, Go, Go…

Dan :)

No Never!

"If you're truly determined to succeed you will! Those that NEVER give up transform dreams into realities!" - *Anonymous*

I love the depiction of the frog in the throat of the bird, the frog's hands are wrapped around the birds throat, the caption says, "never give up". It is so true for me personally; I am determined to win each and every day of my life. Some days are better than others but there is no quit in me. I believe that those of us that have walked the path of destruction as alcoholics or addicts know how to survive the un-survivable!

We are survivors! In recovery however we need to be Thrivers! We need to thrive in the face of uncertainty and challenges. We need to put our head down and do the work that it takes to recover. We need to be bold and win; we are powerful human beings that have the ability to be outstanding in the face of adversity. We have the key and the key is a true reliance upon God.

Go, Go, Go...

Dan :)

Take Action

Inaction breeds doubt and fear. Action breeds confidence and courage. If you want to conquer fear, do not sit home and think about it. Go out and get busy. *-- Dale Carnegie*

Fear paralyzes the best of us. When it comes to alcoholism and addiction more often than not neither the addict nor the family members heed the signs that something is awry early on. Often fear of taking any action paralyzes them into hoping beyond hope that it is going to get better, somehow.

For the addict it is all they know. They justify their use; they do all they can to minimize the challenges they face due to their use. But in the end if they are afflicted with the "creature" they continue to sink deeper into addiction.

For the family, they just want to believe that it is going to get better. That by some miraculous act of God their loved one is just going to stop! They are going to get through their phase and get on with their lives.

Without action nothing changes. Hoping is not action, praying is a start. For the addict an evaluation of how far it has gone and seeking an expert's advice on a plan of action is necessary. For the family, an evaluation of the situation and seek expert advice on how to bring the message to their loved one in a way that elicits positive action.

Finally, when the steps are apparent take definitive action. Recovery requires making the decision to recover. What does recovery entail? It starts with complete abstinence, followed by change. We must change how we think if we are going to find joy. How we think about life, family, friends, alcohol, drugs, and what we really want out of our lives.

Recovery is possible for the family and the addict. But not without decisive action!

Go, Go, Go…

Dan ☺

Preparation

I've never run into a guy who could win at the top level in anything today and didn't have the right attitude, didn't give it everything he had, at least while he was doing it; wasn't prepared and didn't have the whole program worked out. *-- Ted Turner*

Getting prepared, having an attitude of gratitude, planning, and focus on what you are becoming makes recovery and life better and better and better by the day. It gives you that extra ounce of courage when the tough times hit. It allows you to dream about your future. Too many of us come into the recovery process beat up internally, with an expectation of losing again. We slowly transition to an expectation of just getting by, but if we focus on the right things for the right reasons we begin to change and we begin to win.

We start to develop a positive mindset and we begin to realize we are worth it. Life is good and we deserve to give it all we have. We start to realize that we are not our past we are who we are becoming, clean, sober, happy, joyous and productive members of life!

Go, Go, Go...

Dan :)

Risk

"There came a time when the risk to remain tight in the bud was more painful than the risk it took to bloom." -- *Anais Nin*

In the Hall of Fame audio "The Strangest Secret", Earl Nightingale states the number one problem in society today is that people fail to think! They simply don't think. There is a propensity to simply ride with the tide and let life happen. In recovery we must change the way we think. We must take the risk to think outside the box. We must bloom into the people we are meant to be.

Addiction rips us apart at the core. Playing it safe is no longer a viable option. We must seize the day, and seize the opportunity to grow. We do this by changing how we think. We cannot allow time to pass and one-day wake up when our lives have passed us by. We are free from addiction to do something special in life. Recovery is not just abstinence; abstinence is the beginning of recovery. Be a thinker, grow and fulfill your potential, because Life is Good!!!

Go, Go, Go...

Dan :)

Discover The Winner Within You

Twenty years from now you will be more disappointed by the things that you didn't do than by the ones you did do. So throw off the bowlines. Sail away from the safe harbor. Catch the trade winds in your sails. Explore. Dream. Discover. -- *Mark Twain*

Discover the winner within you. Each and everyone one of us have a competitive drive and the winner deep inside of us. Have you ever listened to people gossip about another person? They compare themselves and how they see themselves to the other person. That is competitiveness. I was talking to this heavyset gal once and she said, "If I ever get that fat shoot me", speaking of another gal that was heavier than she.

The point is that we are all competitive; we are all seeking the win! It is always there in some way shape or form. Now I am not suggesting the comment made was a productive one but the point is, there is pride and competitiveness inside us all. Many folks deny this fact; they compare competitiveness to sports and do not see themselves that way.

We need to embrace the winner within us and not fight it off with an attitude of complacency. Complacency is death. Do not allow you to be complacent, do not go twenty years and find yourself living in regret. Go for it, be a healthy positive competitive individual, the winner that you are!!!

Go, Go, Go…

Dan :)

It's Exciting

It is always with excitement that I wake up in the morning wondering what my intuition will toss up to me, like gifts from the sea. I work with it and rely on it. It's my partner. *-- Jonas Salk*

Each and every day holds the potential for an opportunity to grow and expand our lives. Recovery is the second chance we deserve in order to explore our true potential. Andrew Carnegie was once quoted as saying, "we all have two major opportunities in life, is this your first or last?"

We get in life what we give therefore; we need to give all we have to be the best we can be. One of the greatest benefits of mutual support groups is the strength we build by helping others to achieve their goal of recovery. By offering support directly or indirectly we build support, we encourage others and we take the next step we need to move forward in our lives.

The twelve-steps are a guideline for overcoming our challenges and living a spiritual, joy filled life. However, without the fellowship, recovery is tentative at best. We all need others in our lives; none of us has the ability to live socially suppressed. Mutual support whether it is AA, NA, CR, EA, or simply a support group of friends with a common agenda or focus makes the difference.

We get in life what we give, so go share your positive hope for the future. Believe and you will achieve, spread the word!

Go, Go, Go...

Dan :)

Opening Up!

If we skip [step five], we may not overcome drinking. Time after time newcomers have tried to keep to themselves certain facts about their lives. Trying to avoid this humbling experience, they have turned to easier methods. Almost invariably they got drunk. -- *The Big Book*

I struggled with two issues when it came to recovery. The concept of spirituality and the Fifth Step. On the topic of spirituality I was an extremely angry person full of pride and ego. I believed in God but at the same time I did not. I was confused and angry, I asked questions such as, if God existed then why all the suffering in the world? But, I was hurting so much on the inside that I believed I needed to simply stop asking the wrong questions and begin accepting the concept that God "could and would" if I simply allowed Him to do so.

When it came to the Fifth Step however, I was so afraid of considering this principle. In my past if I told the truth about me it always came back to haunt me. I would do anything but tell the truth about my past! One day in a Fifth Step meeting I was deep in thought and excused myself to the men's room. As I walked out my sponsor was at the door. He said, "What is troubling you"? I replied, "nothing, I had to pee", he immediately said, "don't bullshit me what is going on"? I stood and looked at him for a while and finally said, "George, this is the only thing I will not do, I will not do the fifth step! Every time I have told anyone in the past about me it has turned around to hurt me".

I remember it like it was yesterday, George looked me in the eye and said, "What is the worst thing you have ever done in your life"? I stood there shocked thinking, "Did this guy hear me"? He kept looking at me for what seemed like an eternity and once again said, "Come on Danny, what is the worst thing you have ever done? This is your life"! I do not know why, but I blurted it out to him. He smiled and said, "damn we have all been there", and he then told me what he had done equally as crazy.

Honestly, I felt like the weight of the world came off my shoulders. I felt a part of life, I felt a part of recovery and quite frankly in hindsight it was the turning point in my life. Today I am blessed by that simple act of faith in my sponsor and the program. Today I believe I am free of addiction due to taking action on step five! Life is good!

Go, Go, Go…

Dan :)

H.O.W.

Very early in my recovery I learned the acronym, H.O.W. it stands for Honesty, Open-mindedness, and Willingness. Recovery is living a happy, prosperous, clean and sober life. Utilizing the tools of recovery like the Twelve Steps, Power of Positive Thinking, the Law of Attraction, Life's One Law as well as others is the key to attaining a happy and prosperous life. A Recovered Life!

Open-mindedness and Willingness are crucial aspects of the recovery process. Breaking the habit of deciding the outcome of any suggestion prior to investigation is strongly suggested. People are conditioned to think "No" right out of the box. So how does one stay open to the suggestions? It starts with developing the habit of asking different questions. The Big Book of Alcoholics Anonymous suggests "Restraint of Tongue and Pen". I remember attending a fire prevention class with my son Liam. The fireman taught the children to "Stop, Drop and Roll" if they are caught on fire. Similarly developing the habit to "Stop and Think" before we say "No" takes practice. We must Detox our Thoughts. Toxic thoughts paralyze our potential happiness.

Here are some tips:

- Ask questions that seek the positive for instance:
  - Am I limiting myself by not attempting this suggestion?
  - Why am I rejecting this suggestion?
  - Have I truly given my best shot?
  - What is right about this suggestion?
- Use a notepad to weigh out the positives and negatives by writing them down.
- Look at the perspective that maybe you missed something in the past if you have heard the suggestion before.
- Always bounce the idea or suggestion off another informed person.
- Guard your mind watch what goes in to your head. Do not allow negativity to permeate your life.
- Be aware of bitterness. If you have a resentment talk it out. A resentment is like swallowing poison and expecting the other person to die!

- Decide what you want in life and focus on that.
- Believe that your best days are ahead of you, do not worry about past harms.
- Change your vocabulary:
  - Problems = Challenges
  - Have to = Want to
  - Setback = Opportunity for Comeback

I have learned that we are all different. We all learn, act, react, do, and are different people. As carriers of the message of hope and recovery we cannot lock ourselves into a box that shuts people out. Thomas Edison once said, "There are no rules around here we are trying to get something done". Adopt this policy into your thinking. Life is a journey; enjoy the journey clean and sober.

Go, Go, Go…

Dan ☺

The Process

Thinking is easy, acting is difficult, and to put one's thoughts into action is the most difficult thing in the world. — *Johann von Goethe*

 As time goes on in the recovery process I have learned more and more about myself and the challenges that I and most of us face in the process of life. I have learned not to judge others, yet at times I find myself on the throne of judgment. I have learned to be prudent yet at times I find myself compulsive. I have learned to trust yet at times I worry. The list goes on as does the lessons…

As I get better, life gets better.

Go, Go, Go…

Dan :)

Show Up and Suit Up

The investor of today does not profit from yesterday's growth. —
Warren Buffet

Life requires that every day we show up and suit up. Yesterday's growth
can be quickly diminished by today's actions. Each and every day we
must put one foot in front of the other and live the life we are shaping.
Reverting back to old behaviors and repeating past mistakes can stunt your
growth if you do not pick up and dust off immediately. This is the essence
of Step Ten, Take a daily inventory and when we "are" wrong promptly
admit it and amend the actions.

Of course, I am sure Warren Buffet was thinking of this when he was
quoted on growth! Life is good!

Go, Go, Go…

Dan :)

Success

"You have brains in your head.
You have feet in your shoes.
You can steer yourself any direction you choose." --Dr. Seuss

Success is the attainment of a worthy Goal or ideal. The self-development industry seems to focus on the attainment of money as the determining factor for success. This is not a black and white phenomenon I am speaking about. It is implied in the message that the marketers use to get you to buy their self-improvement materials. Why? Because as much as "sex sells" so does making money! Creating massive wealth. Living the life of a rock star without the fame! People spend millions of dollars annually on audio packets, seminars, webinars, videos, and systems and on and on and on…

Successful recovery is the attainment of a worthy goal or ideal. Living a sober and prosperous life focused on two objectives: 1) Your family and personal goals. 2) Giving back to the still suffering and recently recovered addict & or alcoholic.

Self-improvement is at the heart of success. Life is Good!

Go, Go, Go…

Dan ☺

Growing Up

"Please… tell me who you are and what you want. And if you think those are simple questions, keep in mind that most people live their entire lives without arriving at an answer." -- Gary Zukav

Recovery is about growing up and living life on purpose. In order to live a life of purpose we must answer the age-old questions, "who am I, what am I here for"? However, we cannot focus our thoughts on these perplexing and often confusing questions. We must live life one day at a time, work the principles of recovery and address our core beliefs as we go. Keeping it simple but being ever remindful that our lives are more than simply grinding it out day by day.

Life is meant to be enjoyed we find enjoyment in living in congruence with our core beliefs while having fun. It is important to work hard yet it is equally as important to play hard as well. When we work hard, play hard and slowly find our purpose in life, we live life to the fullest! No regrets!!!

Go, Go, Go…

Dan :)

Positive and Negative

"People are defeated by easy, victorious and cheap successes more than by adversity." -- *Benjamin Disraeli*

In early recovery we must be diligent of both sides of the coin the positive and the negative. We are extremely sensitive in the early stages of the process. Sometimes it is the broken shoelace that sends us over the edge. Other times it is a successful fete that leads us to celebrate inappropriately and we end up immersed into addiction again!

Remaining diligent and recognizing that utilizing the tools for recovery will only enhance a successful recovery experience.

Life is good!

Go, Go, Go…

Dan :)

Implementation

"Character isn't inherited. One builds it daily by the way one thinks and acts, thought by thought, action by action. If one lets fear or hate or anger take possession of the mind, they become self-forged chains."
-- Helen Douglas

Implementing the Steps is much more than just taking the Steps! I have worked with folks that take the Steps as if they are a duty or a badge of honor that has been accomplished. Then there are those that implement the steps into their daily lives. Steps 10, 11, and 12 are the daily compilation of Steps 1 through 9. When we live with insight, and take action based upon these principles we build character.

Every time we implement Step 10, where we make amends immediately, we move further away from the behavior that caused the negative action we took. As we implement these disciplines into our lives we begin to live happy, joyous and free. We no longer carry resentment and pent up anger towards others. Yes we get angry but we learn to eradicate the anger through the principles of action we take! Life is good!

Go, Go, Go…

Dan :)

The Creature

By every form of self-deception and experimentation, [real alcoholics] will try to prove themselves exceptions to the rule .... -- *Alcoholics Anonymous, 4th ed., pg. 31*

 Alcoholism and addiction are cunning, baffling and powerful! Quite frankly, for those of us that have the "Creature" it owns us when we are in it! We justify, rationalize and attempt to hold onto them until we simply can no longer do so! Yet some of us never quite get to that place. I pray for them!

For those of us that escape the grip of addiction, we have been blessed with the gift of recovery. Living the recovered life offers us hope for the future. We are no longer chained to the bottle or drug. We are free to make choices in our lives. Life is good!

Go, Go, Go…

Dan :)

Emotional Rescue

"Never apologize for showing feeling. When you do so, you apologize for truth." – *Benjamin Disraeli*

Many of us were taught to not show our emotions. As we grow in our recovery we learn that our emotions are real and they represent how we actually are feeling. We begin to recognize that showing our feelings to one another is acceptable. What we must learn is that we cannot live on emotion alone. We must grow emotionally; and our emotional intelligence must stabilize. We cannot live reactionary lives but we must not be machines either!

Life is about balance. The recovered life takes diligence coupled with balance! Live, life, strong!

Go, Go, Go…

Dan :)

WHY?

"The thing is, we have to let go of all blame, all attacking, all judging, to free our inner selves to attract what we say we want. Until we do, we are hamsters in a cage chasing our own tails and wondering why we aren't getting the results we seek." — *Dr. Joe Vitale*

We live in a society that seemingly encourages blame. Watch the 24-hour News shows and the Sunday Morning Spin Doctors! The Republicans blame the Democrats and vice versa. When something goes wrong in life we always ask, "WHY"? When someone dies of a heart attack the funeral talk is always, bot he/she were too young. They just didn't take care of themselves, they smoked, drank etc… It is a natural occurrence our brains search for meaning and we seek truth or at the very least, the "WHY"!

To live a happy productive life we must learn to live in the "NOW". I am what I am based upon a number of factors, if I am not satisfied with who I am at this moment I can change. Blame, remorse or regret has no place in striving for joy! It simply is, therefore I focus on what I want, where I want to go and who I want to be as a productive member of my family, community and society. Anything less will leave you wagging your tail in disgust! Life is good!

Go, Go, Go…

Dan :)

Resolve!

What if you could be anything, or anybody, you chose to be? Think about it. What would you choose to be? *—Nido Qubein*

I have reflected on all of the chatter about making "New Year Resolutions". As I read through each one of them I thought, "why do people make these, they simply do not work". I did not read one blog or article that shed any positive light on this practice, not one! Made me wonder!

The question I have is what is the truth? Do I believe that resolutions do not work? No, No, and HELL No! Resolutions do work and they work well. But, and this is a huge but, only if they are committed to. That is it; if I simply make a resolution it is only a wish or a hope. I have not resolved to follow through. I have not made a true commitment. I have not made the decision to keep my commitment to myself.

The truth is I can do anything; I can be anybody I chose to be! I have options and so do you! I can search out the options; decide which I will commit to, resolve to follow through and DO IT! I must cut off all other options, especially the big option of "QUIT" and just DO IT! Nothing more and nothing less! Life is good!

Go, Go, Go…

Dan :)

Action

Inaction breeds doubt and fear. Action breeds confidence and courage. If you want to conquer fear, do not sit home and think about it. Go out and get busy. *-- Dale Carnegie*

When it comes to recovery action is the key. We must take action; we must live our lives proactively. It is so much more than just not drinking or drugging. We take the necessary steps to recover, we live the principles of recovery. Keeping our side of the street clean is essential. Steps ten, eleven and twelve are action steps we take on a daily basis.

We begin to live proactively, we lose the "'T" that is the apostrophe "T". We stop looking fro what we can"T do and begin taking action on the things we can do. We are no longer don"T--ers we are DOERS! We take action; we look at life as an adventure. We seek out opportunities to help others like we have been helped! We live with confidence and courage! Life is good!

Go, Go, Go…

Dan :)

Pay the Price

"Let us remember that, as much has been given us, much will be expected from us, and that true homage comes from the heart as well as from the lips, and shows itself in deeds." -- *Theodore Roosevelt*

Recovery does come with a price tag, not only the price of admission, i.e. getting sober you must pay the price, and it takes work. To stay sober we must pay the price by helping others to attain the same. Recovery is a gift, in the beginning it may not seem that way and it sounds like an oxymoron. It feels more like a loss of "the fun" or the "party". But as we grow we realize that if we continued to drink and or drug we are destined to live a life of continued unpredictability at best.

For me personally I was miserable and living a life of quiet desperation. I was sick and tired of living the way I was living. People that thought I was having fun surrounded me, but the truth is that inside I was dead. I was willing to pay the price to recover. Today I am grateful that I followed the people that put their hand out to me. The people that told me it was worth it! Today I attempt to do the same.

Life is good!

Go, Go, Go…

Dan ☺

If Not NOW, When?

"The great Western disease is, 'I'll be happy when… When I get the money. When I get a BMW. When I get this job.' Well, the reality is, you never get to when. The only way to find happiness is to understand that happiness is not out there. It's in here. And happiness is not next week. It's now." – *Marshall Goldsmith*

It is so easy to get caught up in the, "I will be OK when" syndrome. I remember in my early recovery feeling that way often. When I get through this, when I get through the steps, when I get a better job, when I get a nice apartment, when, when, when… As frustrating as it seems in the beginning it is better than the alternative, "Frig It"!

As we progress in our recovery and life we learn how to deal with the emotional roller coaster of "when". We learn that our happiness is here and now. The journey is up and down but we do not need to live emotionally up and down.

I went through a stage that I wanted reasonable happiness. But I quickly learned that happiness is happiness and I did not need to put a limit on my joy. I wanted to protect myself from let down as if I would never find true happiness. I was wrong, when I finally let go and began to live in joy; joy remained, "Within"! Life is good!

Go, Go, Go…

Dan

Conclusion

Once again I want to thank you for taking the time to read and hopefully learn and internalize the lessons in each of these essays. Life is a journey and recovery is part of life for those of us that choose it. Stay strong, live life with passion. Take each and every day as an opportunity to get better and better and better. This book has started you off in the right direction. I truly believe that if we take our recovery seriously we have the chance to do something special with our lives. But we must have the heart of a champion. My personal Mission is to offer people with addictions a chance to build a life they are proud of and to gain independence for themselves and their families. In conclusion here are some points to ponder:

* If we have "heart and drive", and want to do something great with our lives, we need to dream again, set goals and become what we are capable of becoming.

* To accomplish something great in this world; we must have a purpose! Service is purpose. People ARE the future and how you treat people will determine your success or failure as a human being.

* The only qualification for success is a 'burning desire' to succeed and a 'will to win.' **"If you think you can win or if you think you can't, you're right."** *Henry Ford.* What is a Burning desire? Your healthy pride and a healthy ego, as you aim to reach your potential!

* Recognize that life will eventually turn out for you the way you see it turning out. You must see good things happening again. You must like yourself again. You must be excited about life again.

* Know that it takes Work!!! "Nothing worth having comes easy. People must recognize the fact that big dreams have big prices. Then determine the price you're willing to pay for success and do it! Recovery is work. Actually the recovery foundation is the hardest work. It starts with a Decision, which creates your commitment.

* To RECOVER we must start by Thinking Differently, we must have a shift in our assumptions about life.

* What does it mean to think differently? First we must recognize that we see the world from our own perspective. We need to create a new perspective. To live in balance we need to be aware of as many points of view as possible. We do this by Gathering all the Data, we cannot be prudent with only half the info!

* Read often, listen to audio books and educational audio sets. Make your car a learning library. Fill your IPod with positive educational and motivational audios, and listen to them at least half the time you use it.

* Remember this; Attitude is everything. The dictionary says attitude is "a matter of bearing or mood". Attitude sets the stage for what we want or expect to happen. An attitude that demands excellence attains excellence. If you expect failure you will get failure. If you expect and settle for nothing less than excellence; you will attain excellence. Contrary to

popular belief we are not born with a great attitude, it takes work. The quality of our attitude comes from learning or experience. Therefore you can relearn and create the experience now.

* We are here for just a flicker of time. Before you know it, it is over! Get it done don't quit on your self! Be a champion!

Again thank you and keep the faith! It is worth it!

Your friend,

Dan Callahan ☺

www.HappyRecovery.com
www.Rehabs.org
www.Rehab-Programs.org
Dan@rehabs.org